WRAP YOUR ARMS AROUND ME

PATRICIA RODDEN HENDERZAHS

WestBow Press books may be ordered through booksellers or by contacting:

WestBow Press
A Division of Thomas Nelson & Zondervan
1663 Liberty Drive
Bloomington, IN 47403
www.westbowpress.com
844-714-3454

Interior Image Credit: Salvador Capuyan

ISBN: 978-1-6642-2854-2 (sc)
ISBN: 978-1-6642-2915-0 (hc)
ISBN: 978-1-6642-2855-9 (e)

Library of Congress Control Number: 2021906069

Print information available on the last page.

WestBow Press rev. date: 3/29/2021

WESTBOW
PRESS®
A DIVISION OF THOMAS NELSON
& ZONDERVAN

For my grandchildren, Ben, Jack, Ella and Chloe
May you always feel God's arms
wrapped around you.

Wrap your arms around me, God, and keep me safe and warm.
For in your arms, oh God, I know that I am safe from harm.

You helped me laugh.

You helped me cry.

You helped me when I asked you, "Why?"

You helped me run, play, jump, and hide

and when it rained, to be inside.

I've learned to listen, watch, and grow.

And someday soon, I hope to know more of your world, the moon, the seas,

the winds that blow.

I've grown in knowledge, skill, and love.

And with your blessings from above,
I'll learn to trust and know and be.

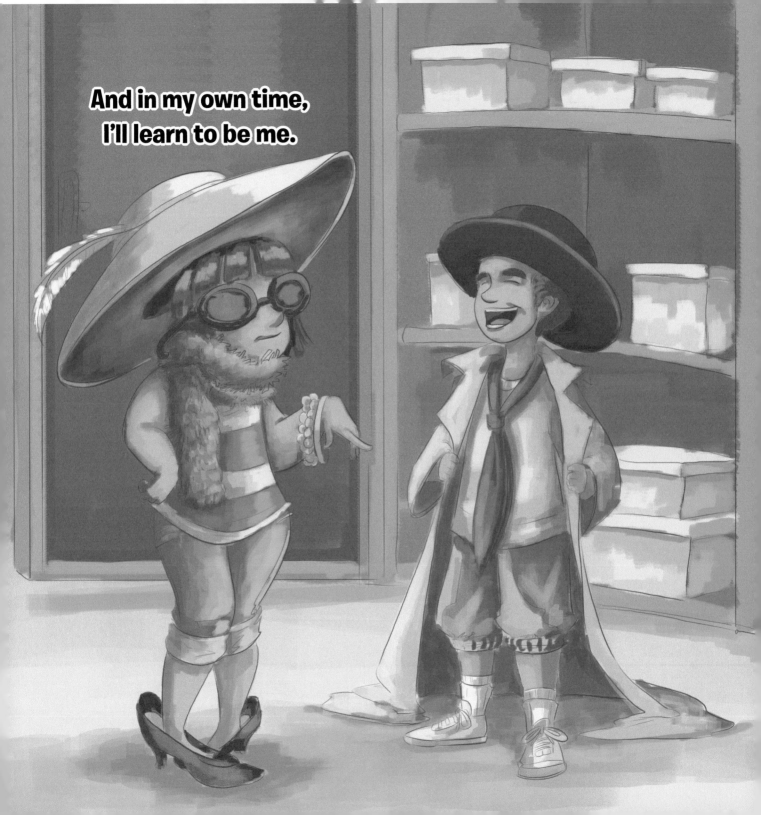

I'll make those I love
so proud of me.

Please teach me love . . . and kindness . . . to share,

to grow in your world,

to show others I care.

Thank you, God, for this day.

Wrap your arms around me and keep me safe
and healthy till the new day is here.

Amen.